STAN LEE

STAN LEE

COMIC BOOK SUPERHERO

by Martin Gitlin

Content Consultant:
Kelley J. Hall
Associate Professor of Sociology, DePauw University

ABDO
Publishing Company

CREDITS

Published by ABDO Publishing Company, 8000 West 78th Street, Edina, Minnesota 55439. Copyright © 2010 by Abdo Consulting Group, Inc. International copyrights reserved in all countries. No part of this book may be reproduced in any form without written permission from the publisher. The Essential Library™ is a trademark and logo of ABDO Publishing Company.

Printed in the United States.

Editor: Mari Kesselring
Copy Editor: Paula Lewis
Interior Design and Production: Nicole Brecke
Cover Design: Nicole Brecke

Library of Congress Cataloging-in-Publication Data
Gitlin, Marty.
  Stan Lee : comic book superhero / by Martin Gitlin.
     p. cm.—(Essential lives)
  Includes bibliographical references and index.
  ISBN 978-1-60453-702-4
  1. Lee, Stan—Juvenile literature. 2. Cartoonists—United States—Biography—Juvenile literature. I. Title.
  PN6727.L39Z65 2009
  741.5092--dc22
  [B]
                                         2008055526

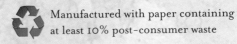

Stan Lee

TABLE OF CONTENTS

Stan Lee in 2008

THE TURNING POINT

Stan Lee was bored. He was tired of writing comic books featuring monsters, which were so common in the late 1950s. He was angry with his publisher's restrictions that prevented him from using his creativity and new ideas. He was impatient with the consumers, who did not seem to want anything different. Lee yearned to explore new territory in his writing, but he felt like a lone wolf in the wilderness. The world of comic books was going nowhere and so was he.

It was 1960, and Stan Lee was planning to quit his job with Atlas Comics. He was considering leaving the profession entirely. Even though he had found success as a comic book writer, he was not happy. Ideas for new characters and stories were fermenting in his mind, but neither his editors nor the buying public were allowing him to create them.

Lee took action. He did not resign from Atlas, but he did not resign himself to professional frustration, either. He had always spent his hours away from work pursuing freelance writing jobs. And with the new decade, he had created a humor book titled *Blushing Blurbs.* He wrote funny fictional quotes and attributed them to people in photos. He followed it up with a similar book called *Golfers Anonymous.* The work soothed his

You Don't Say

One of the projects Lee pursued in the early 1960s was a magazine titled *You Don't Say.* Lee wrote funny quote lines for photos of famous people.

The third issue featured President John F. Kennedy on the cover. But just as it was about to go on sale, Kennedy was assassinated. Atlas Comics certainly could not joke about a dead president. Every copy of the issue was quickly removed from the market. But despite this setback, Lee returned to writing political humor later in his career.

Stan Lee wrote for Atlas Comics.

frustration for a short time. But one day in 1961, a friendly golf game that Lee was not even involved in would change his life.

The golfers were Atlas publisher Martin Goodman and his counterpart Jack Liebowitz at National Periodicals, later called DC Comics. The two men were friendly rivals on the golf course and in business. During their game, Liebowitz mentioned to Goodman that a comic book about a superhero team featuring Superman, Batman, and Wonder Woman called *The Justice League of America* was selling very well.

Goodman stored that tidbit of information in the back of his mind. When he returned to work, he called Lee into his office. "Maybe we ought to do some superheroes," Goodman suggested.[1] Amazingly, this was the day Lee had planned to inform Goodman that he was leaving the company. But even with Goodman's enthusiasm, Lee was skeptical. Goodman's suggestion prevented him from leaving Atlas Comics that day, but he still planned to quit the following day. Little did Lee know that he was about to revive his career. He would change the face of the comic book industry with the launch of what would become known as the Marvel Age of Comics.

A New Philosophy

Lee believed that comic book superheroes of the previous decades, such as Superman and Wonder Woman, were one-dimensional. They boasted powers such as superhuman strength or the ability to fly, but they did not face any real-life problems like Stan Lee had faced in his life. Lee thought superheroes needed a human touch. He believed they should have weaknesses as well as strengths.

They should bicker and argue; they should feel resentment and even depression.

Lee's ideas would not matter, though, now that he was going to quit. He spoke that night with his wife, Joan. She told her husband:

> If Martin wants you to create a new group of superheroes, this could be a chance for you to do it the way you've always wanted to. You could dream up plots that have more depth and substance to them, and create characters who have interesting personalities, who speak like real people . . . . The worst that can happen is that Martin will get mad and fire you; but you want to quit anyway, so what's the risk?[2]

Joan's words convinced Lee to stay at Atlas Comics.

"The World's Greatest Comic Magazine"

In an effort to market *The Fantastic Four*, Lee put a motto on the cover of each comic book. He placed the words "The World's Greatest Comic Magazine" on each issue. It seemed bold at the time, but few would argue with that claim when it became one of the most popular series in comic book history.

THE START OF SOMETHING BIG

Lee set out to create a comic book unlike any other on the market. He wrote about a group of four people who leave Earth in a rocket ship and are hit by cosmic rays. Upon their return, they discover that the rays have given them incredible powers. The Fantastic Four were born.

Each member of the Fantastic Four had different powers. Reed Richards, who was Mr. Fantastic, could bend and stretch himself into superhuman shapes. Susan Storm was the Invisible Girl. She boasted the power to make herself invisible. Johnny Storm, or the Human Torch, created flames of fire and could fly. Ben Grimm was called the Thing. He developed incredible strength. Most importantly, however, the Fantastic Four were a family. Richards was engaged to Susan Storm, whose younger brother was Johnny Storm. Grimm was a friend to each of them.

Lee broke all the rules. Superheroes had always been good-natured

Where Is Latveria?

The job was not complete after Stan Lee created the superheroes of the Fantastic Four. He still needed a super villain. Enter Dr. Victor von Doom.

Lee created von Doom to be as smart as Reed Richards and driven by one goal in life: to conquer the world. What Lee found interesting about that desire was that it is not illegal. He explained that he could declare to a police officer that he wished to conquer the world and he could not be arrested. Dr. Doom's desire to take over the world created an endless number of plot possibilities for Lee's fertile imagination.

Only one task remained for Lee in creating Dr. Doom. He needed to determine where Dr. Doom was from. Lee considered various places before coming up with a fictional country named Latveria. He made Dr. Doom king of Latveria. Lee embraced the notion that as king of another country, Dr. Doom could wreak havoc in America and not get into trouble for it. Over the years, Dr. Doom has become one of the most despised of all comic book villains.

and handsome, but the Thing was volatile and grotesque looking. The Human Torch enjoyed playing jokes on his friends such as burning their toes. Females had generally been minor characters in comic books, but Invisible Girl was as important as the other three. Superheroes were known for being modest and exciting, but Mr. Fantastic was conceited and dull.

Recycling a Character

Atlas publisher Martin Goodman tried to make the brainstorming of a new team of superheroes easy on Lee. Goodman suggested that Lee use his older creations such as the Human Torch and Captain America for the project. Lee took his advice about the Human Torch, but he drastically changed the character. The other three of the Fantastic Four were new characters.

After Lee wrote the initial script of *The Fantastic Four*, artist Jack Kirby brought the characters to life. Lee was thrilled by the way Kirby drew the superheroes and tied the visuals with the stories. But Lee also believed his publisher would object to the entire concept.

The first issue of *The Fantastic Four* was released in November 1961. Sales skyrocketed. Fan mail poured in. The industry had been transformed, and readers could thank Lee for it. And Lee still had more ahead of him. He would soon produce a string of characters that would be cherished by fans for generations. ⌐

Cover of The Fantastic Four #1

Stanley was born in New York City in 1922.

STANLEY AND HIS SPACESHIP BIKE

The comic book, as it is known today, had yet to be created when Stanley Martin Lieber was born on December 28, 1922. Stanley's parents were Jack and Celia Lieber. They were Jewish immigrants. They had traveled from Romania to the United States to seek a better life in the early twentieth century.

Like many of the Jewish immigrants in America's largest city, Jack toiled in the garment district. He worked as a dress cutter. But even before the Great Depression sent the nation's economy tumbling, Jack struggled to find employment. Jack's problems intensified when the stock market crashed in 1929. He could not find a job. Though still a small boy, Stanley suffered as well. He could not understand why a man who wanted to work could not.

The Liebers grew poorer each year. To save money, they moved to an apartment that was so tiny that Stanley slept on the living room couch instead of a bed in a bedroom of his own. The only sight to be seen from the windows of his new home was the building next door.

The stress took a toll on Jack. He argued constantly with his wife about money, and he became more demanding of his son. Stanley often sought out the love of his mother, Celia, who was far kinder and more nurturing.

Walt Disney

One of Stanley's early role models was Walt Disney. Disney created Mickey Mouse in 1928 long before becoming the most famous cartoon animator in the world. As a child, Stanley enjoyed watching the Disney cartoon shorts in movie theaters before the featured attractions.

Stanley, left, lived with his parents and his younger brother in New York City.

The birth of Stanley's brother Larry in 1931 added additional financial pressure to the Lieber family. Jack searched in vain for steady work well into the decade. He would scour the want ads in the paper or shuffle down the street in an attempt to find jobs that would feed his wife and children.

Getting Away from It All

Stanley spent his free time seeking out diversions as an escape from the despair that gripped his family. His favorites were books and movies. Stanley rarely could afford the 25 cents required for admission into the movie theater. But when he did scrape up enough money, he would sit spellbound as he watched swashbuckling stars of the day such as Errol Flynn.

Radio programs also served to calm the family and provide much-needed entertainment. The Liebers would arrange chairs in a semicircle around the radio and laugh at the antics of Jack Benny and other comedians of that era.

Stanley enjoyed newspaper comic strips as well, though not as much as one might think considering his future career. But he was an avid reader from early childhood. His mother would joke that if there were nothing else on hand to read, he would read ketchup bottles.

First Comics

One day, Stanley picked up a pencil and let his imagination run wild. Little did he know that it would be the start of a love affair with character creation and story writing that would remain with him for the rest of his life. He recalled,

> *I began scribbling little illustrated stories to amuse myself. I would draw a straight horizontal line for the horizon and then add stick figures above it, around which I built simple stories and plot lines. I was, without knowing it, creating my first [comic books]. This was a make-believe world I loved.*[2]

Stanley did not need to read or to draw to create an imaginary world for himself. He could get the same effect by hopping on his bicycle. As he pedaled through the streets, he imagined he

Reading Shakespeare

Many children and young teenagers read the works of the famous playwright and poet William Shakespeare in school. Stanley Lieber began reading Shakespeare on his own.

Stanley started reading Shakespeare's plays and poetry at the age of ten. He liked the way the words sounded when he read them aloud. He later explained,

> *While I'm sure that most of [Shakespeare's] work was way over my then juvenile head, I was fascinated by the rhythm of the words, by the flowery language, the "What ho, Horatio" type of outpourings. The same with the Bible. Though I'm not particularly religious, I love that style of writing . . . the "thees" and "thous" and "begats," which can make the simplest thought seem fraught with drama.*[1]

It seems that young Stanley's reading had an effect on his style of writing when he began to write comic books. One of his early creations is a comic book about a Norse god named Thor. Shakespearian language is strongly represented in Thor's speech.

was a space man on a spaceship about to blast off to the moon. Because his family was too poor to own a car, Stanley needed his bike not only to fire his imagination, but also to reach places too far to walk.

A Boost in Confidence

When he was only 15 years old, Stanley received the first validation of his talent as a writer. He entered a student contest called "The Biggest News of the Week." The contest was run by the *New York Herald Tribune*, one of the many newspapers in the city at the time.

The competition required students to write a short essay about what they believed to be the most important news item of the week. The top seven entries were given cash awards. Stanley entered on several occasions, finishing seventh once and earning two honorable mention prizes. Considering that thousands of kids participated, the honors gave him confidence and directed his ambitions toward a writing career.

From Stanley Lieber to Stan Lee

During his high school days, Stanley wrote for the student magazine. One day, he noticed that a man painting the ceiling of the magazine office had left his ladder in the middle of the room. Taking the opportunity to clown around, Stanley climbed the ladder and wrote the words "Stan Lee is God" on the ceiling.[3] Even Stan Lee cannot remember if this was the first time that he used what would later become his pen name. But it was a name that would serve him well when he started writing comic books.

Two of Stanley's school-
mates also went into the
comic book business.
Bob Kane and Bill Finger
created the popular com-
ic book series *Batman* for
DC Comics. Finger wrote
the comics while Kane
did the illustrations.

DC Comics had
already found success
with their *Superman* comics when they contacted
artist Bob Kane about
creating a new superhero.
Kane then collaborated
with Finger to create the
Batman character. The
new *Batman* comics
had a darker tone than
the *Superman* comics.
When writing the comics,
Finger looked to horror
stories and gangster films
as examples. Kane's illustrations included heavy
shadows and strange
angles to help achieve
this darker tone.

By that time, he was one of
10,000 students at DeWitt Clinton,
one of the largest and most diverse
schools in the country. Stanley's
classmates were Irish, Italian, Jewish,
and African-American children,
many of whom were the children
of immigrants as well. Previous
graduates of the school included
Batman cocreators Bob Kane and Bill
Finger.

After only a year at DeWitt
Clinton, Stanley had gained a
reputation for his friendliness,
talent, and outgoing personality.
"You always knew that he was going
to be successful," said high school
friend Bob Wendlinger, who later
had a writing career of his own.
"It was a given."[2]

Soon Stanley's uncle had an idea. He believed he
knew of an outlet for Stanley's writing talent. And
after the teenager followed through with his uncle's
advice, the comic book world would never be the
same.

Stanley always had a big imagination.

At Timely Comics, Lee met art director Jack Kirby.

PLANTING THE SEEDS

Many high school graduates look forward
to attending college. Stan Lee was
not so fortunate. When Lee graduated in 1939,
his family could not afford to send him to college.
Instead, Lee found a job to help his family.

Though many of the negative effects of the Great Depression had lessened by then, some people in the United States still felt financial hardship. And Lee's family was among them.

Lee held several small jobs during high school and shortly after graduation. One of the toughest was as an errand boy for salesmen at a pants manufacturer. He jumped up and fetched whatever was needed, which he felt to be humiliating. He was relieved when the company fired him after a few weeks.

He still yearned to be a writer, but at age 17, he did not know how to get into that field. Luckily, Robbie Solomon, his mother's brother, had an idea. Solomon knew of a job opening at Timely Comics, owned by another relative, Martin Goodman. Goodman was married to Lee's cousin. Lee decided to check it out and was delighted to discover that Timely published comic books. He also learned that Timely was planning to start a new comic book titled *Captain America Comics*. But to his

City College

Lee eventually did attend a college for a short time. He enrolled at City College in New York City, mostly to spend more time with a girl he was dating who was also enrolled there. Lee took night courses, but his time there did not last long. When the relationship ended six months later, he quit school.

dismay, Lee found the Timely comics to be poorly written and weakly drawn.

Lee's Big Chance

Lee did not realize it at the time, but that poorly written comic would turn out to be his opportunity. Timely would need to improve the quality of its work, and Lee would eventually be in the forefront of that turnaround. In the process, he would establish relationships with Goodman, editor Joe Simon and, most importantly, art director Jack Kirby. Kirby would later bring many of Lee's most famous creations to life.

All in the Family

Even though Timely publisher Martin Goodman was related to Lee, the two barely knew each other. Goodman was married to Lee's cousin Jean. But since Goodman was several years older than Lee, they spent little time together while Lee was growing up. By the time Lee was in high school, Goodman had already established his business.

Lee's uncle Robbie, who set Lee up with the job at Timely, did not bother telling Goodman that Lee had been hired. According to Lee, Goodman appeared surprised when he saw him in the office. When Lee wrote his autobiography several decades later, he expressed confusion as to whether Goodman's surprise at seeing him at Timely was serious or a joke.

Lee was not the only relative of publisher Martin Goodman to work at Timely—most of Goodman's employees were relations. Goodman's brother Abe ran bookkeeping. Brother Dave took photos for the magazine. Youngest brother Artie handled the comic book color guides. And Robbie, who brought Lee into the company, performed many odd jobs in the office.

However, upon his hiring at Timely for eight dollars a week, Lee did the same work he did at the pants manufacturer. He ran errands. But he was also told that he might eventually be given the chance to write. That was all Lee needed to hear to accept the job.

Soon it was clear that Stan Lee had landed on the ground floor of a blossoming industry. When DC Comics's *Action Comics #1* arrived on the newsstands in 1938, its cover featured a figure in a red and blue costume holding a car over his head. Superman had arrived and was about to change the comic book industry forever.

Dave Berg

Dave Berg was among the artists who worked with Lee at Timely in the 1930s. Berg was not employed for long, but he did make a name for himself. Berg later served as a *Mad Magazine* artist. *Mad Magazine* was a different type of comic book than what Stan Lee usually worked on. It poked fun at aspects of American life. Berg worked for more than 40 years at *Mad*, where he became best known for a strip called *The Lighter Side*, which may have been the magazine's most popular monthly feature.

With Superman leading the way, the monthly circulation of *Action Comics* leaped to 500,000 copies. Batman soon followed. Superheroes were all the rage. As the 1940s began and the United States was about to be drawn into World War II, comic books were flourishing. Timely was destined to benefit from their growing popularity. From staff writer

Carl Burgos emerged the Human Torch, a fire-engulfed creature that Lee later remodeled and included in *The Fantastic Four*. Bill Everett created Sub-Mariner, who ruled over and gained power from the sea and sought revenge on humans for ruining his underwater world.

"Mr. Timely Comics"

By the early 1940s, the German armies led by the Nazi Party had gained control of much of Europe. Germany's campaign to take over the continent fueled the concerns of Americans that the armies might try to invade the United States. In the pages of comic books, superheroes began to battle the enemies of the nation.

Taking advantage of the popularity of such comic book characters, Simon and Kirby created Captain America. On the cover of the first issue of *Captain America Comics*, the title character is shown landing a punch on the jaw of German dictator Adolf Hitler. The character became so popular that *Captain America Comics* sold 1 million copies.

As Timely expanded the number of comic books it produced, the staff became overwhelmed. Lee was given permission to write a two-page piece titled

Many children enjoyed reading comic books in the late 1930s.

"The Traitor's Revenge" that appeared in *Captain America #3* in May 1941. This work received a positive response. Just three months later, he penned his first comic book script for the same magazine. This was also when he began using "Stan Lee" as his pen name. He officially changed his name in the 1970s.

The path to prominence at Timely was further cleared for Lee in 1941. After financial disputes over *Captain America Comics,* both Kirby and Simon left

Timely and worked mainly with DC
Comics. After that, Goodman made
Lee the temporary editorial director.
Lee recalled,

> *In some ways, I was embarrassed to let
> visitors to the office know that I was the
> editor because they might think we weren't
> a serious business if an [18-year-old]
> kid was running the shop. Sometimes I'd
> be in the reception room and some grown-up would come
> in and see me sitting there in my sneakers and sweatshirt and
> say, "Hey, kid, where can I find Mr. Lee?" . . . I knew [he'd]
> be embarrassed if I said, "I'm Mr. Lee." So instead, I'd say,
> "Just a minute, sir, I'll tell him you're here." Then I'd run
> out and call the receptionist, "Tell him Mr. Lee is gone for
> the day."[1]*

Lee wrote and drew dozens of stories. He had his
own office, which made him feel important, and he
produced scripts for *Captain America Comics* as well as
lesser-known superheroes such as the Whizzer, Black
Marvel, and Jack Frost.

But soon, Lee received a call he could not turn
down. It was a call to serve his country.

Stan Lee wrote a two-page piece for Captain America #3.

Stan Lee volunteered for the army in 1942.

WRITER IN WAR, EDITOR IN PEACE

On December 7, 1941, Japanese warplanes attacked Pearl Harbor, a U.S. naval base in Hawaii. The following day, President Franklin Roosevelt announced that the United States was officially in a state of war against Japan. Soon after, the United States declared war against Germany as well.

While millions of young men enlisted in the various branches of the military immediately, others did not join the fight until they were drafted. Some simply waited for what they believed to be the right time.

Stan Lee was not quite ready to enlist in the armed forces in late 1941. He was still a teenager and he had just begun his career in the comic book business. In addition, the comic book industry was expanding in different directions. Humorous comic book characters were gaining on superheroes in popularity.

In 1941, Dell Comics had introduced books featuring Walt Disney and Looney Tunes characters such as Mickey Mouse and Bugs Bunny. Soon Timely published *Joker Comics #1* that featured odd characters such as Dr. Nutzy, Eustice Hayseed, Powerhouse Pepper, and Stuporman, a funny take-off of Superman.

Golden Age of Comics

The period of time from the 1930s into the late 1940s is often called the Golden Age of Comics. During this time period, superhero comics first became popular. Many of them are still well known today. DC Comics introduced Superman, Batman, Wonder Woman, the Flash, Green Lantern, and many others. Timely Comics introduced Captain America, the Human Torch, and Sub-Mariner.

Working Women

When many American men left the workforce to fight in World War II, women stepped up to fill their jobs. The number of women working in the comic book industry tripled during the war. After the war, some of the women continued working at their new jobs. However, as was common with most industries of the time, most of the women workers in the comic book industry were replaced as the men returned from war.

The strong reaction to *Joker Comics* motivated Lee to create *Comedy Comics*. These featured both superhero and humor stories.

Lee, however, felt a sense of patriotism. He could no longer justify writing comic books. Millions of American men were fighting and thousands were dying. He pretended to be heroic, but in reality he was frightened. He said,

I used to go to penny arcades in New York and shoot those little guns and win prizes all the time—I figured I was a shoo-in to handle real guns. . . . I enlisted in the army because I couldn't bear the idea of my being home while other guys my age were fighting. I don't think I could have lived with myself if I hadn't enlisted. To tell you the truth, I was actually kind of scared— but I didn't want to think of myself as a coward or a slacker.[1]

In the Army at Home

Lee indeed believed he could handle a gun, but he did not need to. He never left the United States during World War II. He was assigned to the

Stan Lee wrote and illustrated training manuals and films
for the army during World War II.

communication division of the army, or Signal
Corps, to write and illustrate training manuals and
films. The army sent him to army bases in various
locations, including North Carolina and Indiana,
for the duration of the war. His job description also
included drawing posters that would educate troops
being prepared to fight.

Lee was not alone among comic book writers and
illustrators who put their careers on hold to serve in
the military. Joe Simon, Jack Kirby, Bill Everett, and
Carl Burgos all did the same. That, however, did not

Destined for Fame

Lee was not the only person in the U.S. Army Signal Corps who later gained fame. Frank Capra worked alongside Lee. Capra wrote many screenplays. He also directed famous movies such as *It's a Wonderful Life* and *Mr. Smith Goes to Washington.* Another was cartoonist Charles Addams, who created the Addams Family, which inspired a television series and two movies.

prevent the industry from thriving in the midst of war. Comic books glorifying soldiers appealed to young boys. A new line of comic books such as *Tessie the Typist* and *Junior Miss* geared toward teenage girls were also produced. Publishers were selling an estimated 25 million comic books a month by December 1943.

Lee had not completely separated himself from Timely during the war. He continued to write stories for its comic books, earning as much as $500 in a weekend, which was tremendous pay at the time. But he missed the daily work at Timely. Upon his discharge from the army, he did not take time off before getting back to work.

He returned immediately in 1945 to Timely in New York, where he rented a two-room apartment at the Hotel Almanac. Lee quickly discovered that the comic book business had changed. Readers were losing interest in superheroes. New genres about romance, crime, and the Old West gained popularity. Though Timely was not at the forefront of the changes, it followed the trend.

A New Chapter in Lee's Life

Soon after returning to New York, British hat model Joan Boocock entered Lee's life at a party in the fall of 1947. Lee fell head over heels in love.

There was only one problem—she was married. However, she was not happily married. She had only known her husband for one day before he proposed to her and she accepted. But soon, her love for her husband faltered. Lee, now 25 years old, encouraged Joan to file for divorce. Six weeks later, she did. And just minutes after the divorce was finalized, she and Lee were wed.

Mail Leads to Jail?

A misunderstanding during Lee's stint in the army nearly landed him at Leavenworth—where military personnel who break the law are sent. Lee had been receiving assignments from Timely while he was still in the army. One week he was expecting an assignment from Timely in the mail on Friday. He planned to write his comic book stories and send them back on Tuesday, his deadline.

On Friday, the mail clerk did not mention his name during mail call. Lee was perplexed since Timely usually sent him assignments on time. The next day, he walked by the mailroom and saw an envelope from Timely in his mail slot. The door was locked, so he marched into the office of the mail clerk and demanded that it be opened so he could retrieve his mail. When the clerk refused, Lee took matters into his own hands. He used a screwdriver to work his way into the office and got the letter containing his Timely assignments. He then locked the office back up. He did not think much of it.

But the company commander called Lee into his office the next day and threatened to send him to Leavenworth for breaking into the mailroom. Fortunately, Lee was deemed too important as a writer to be dispatched to the military prison.

Newly married Lee then decided to write a short book about the process of producing a comic book titled *Secrets Behind the Comics*. He included several blank pages so aspiring comic book writers and artists could practice. Lee recommended that young artists spend at least one hour on each blank page.

Lee, however, is the first to admit that the explosion of interest in comic books during that time filled him with greed. He was content to churn out stories that would sell without stopping to ask if he was maximizing his talent. But he knew in the back of his mind that he boasted far more creative ability than he was putting to use in the Timely comic books. Lee said,

> *I was just doing what my publisher asked me to do. Being young, I enjoyed the feeling of importance of being editor and art director and head writer. It never occurred to me that what I was doing wasn't all that great.* [2]

That would soon change, along with just about everything in Lee's life. ⌐

Stan Lee married Joan Boocock.

Comic books were popular in the early 1950s.

TROUBLE IN PARADISE

World War II turned millions of young men into adults. Many had encountered new experiences and challenges while at war. And although Stan Lee was not shipped overseas to fight, his duties still matured him. So did his marriage. His wife, Joan, gave up her modeling and acting career and took care of their household. Lee became the sole financial provider for his family. He knew that Joan depended on him, and he did not take that responsibility lightly.

Lee became a workaholic. He not only wrote comic book scripts at the office, but at home as well—often late into the night. His motivation was not only financial; he wanted to maximize his talents as a comic book writer. Meanwhile, Timely stayed with the current comic book trends and continued to produce crime-related material such as *Official True Crime Cases*, *True Complete Mystery*, *Amazing Detective Cases*, and *Private Eye* through the early 1950s. Lee followed right along.

Even though Lee was not excited about the direction Timely was headed, he had no choice but to continue working. He had more mouths to feed. In 1947, after the death of Lee's mother, his 15-year-old brother Larry moved in and remained until he was old enough to live on his own. In April 1950, Stan and Joan welcomed daughter Joan Celia into the family.

Soon Lee was making enough money to move to a home in a wealthy community in Long Island.

In 1953, Stan and Joan's second daughter, Jan, was born. But, sadly, the baby died three days later. The Lees also learned that Joan could not have any more children.

DR. FREDERIC WERTHAM AND THE COMICS CODE

In the 1950s, Lee became concerned about his job in the comic book industry. Timely, which had become known as Atlas Comics, was doing well. But Lee was still worried. The industry had flourished for more than a decade, but what if it fell out of favor with the public? Who would hire a 30-year-old

Giving a Bit of Advice

In 1947, *Writer's Digest* magazine wanted Lee to give its readers a few words of wisdom. Lee was asked to write the lead article of the November issue, which was titled "There's Money in Comics." Lee was never certain why *Writer's Digest* singled him out to write such an article, which was to be geared toward kids and adults looking for careers as comic book writers.

The cover of the magazine showed Lee with a pipe in his mouth—even though he never smoked a pipe. He believed it would make him look older and more distinguished, but he later wished he had posed without the pipe.

In his article, Lee wrote that prospective comic book writers should keep five points in mind:

1. Write an interesting beginning to the story.
2. Use smooth continuity from panel to panel.
3. Use realistic dialogue because it creates good characterization.
4. Maintain suspense throughout.
5. Provide a satisfying ending.

Those were rules Lee had always followed throughout his career as a comic book writer.

whose only experience was writing stories about superheroes and crime fighters for children?

Soon, some of Lee's fears were realized. A controversy had begun with claims made by Dr. Frederic Wertham, a New York psychiatrist. Wertham claimed that reading comic books motivated young people to commit acts of violence and crime. He argued that many of the disturbed young patients he treated read comic books. Wertham also added his viewpoint that comic book superheroes encouraged children to find joy at seeing people hurt.

Lee had heard these arguments before. He had gone on the offensive in April 1953, when he wrote a story titled "The Raving Maniac" that appeared in *Suspense #29*. Lee recalled the details of the comic,

> I played me [in the story]. . . . In the
> story, I was the head man at a [comic

Marvel Boy

Lee made an unsuccessful attempt to revive super-hero comic books in the early 1950s. He started with a character named Marvel Boy. Although Marvel Boy had super-human strength and could read minds, the comic book lasted for just two issues.

Lee also tried to revive Sub-Mariner, the Human Torch, and Captain America in 1954, but those failed as well. Super-heroes would not become popular again for several years.

**Seduction
of the Innocent**

Dr. Fredric Wertham's *Seduction of the Innocent* was published in 1954. The book was illustrated with panels from comic books. Wertham used these illustrations as evidence for his claims that comic books were bad for children. He included many different types of comics in his study, such as horror, crime, and superhero comics. This study caused a controversy in the comic book industry. However, today most people no longer take Wertham's book seriously because he did not offer any research to support his conclusions.

book] company when suddenly, some nutcase, raving maniac came crashing in to [scream at me] about the evils of [comic books]. . . . The [comic book] executive whom I portrayed lashed back with some of the usual arguments plus a new one or two. . . . Naturally, those points were so powerful in that [comic book] story that the raving maniac slunk off in utter defeat. But that was fiction. I wish we could have dismissed Dr. Frederic Wertham as easily. [1]

Dr. Wertham's 1954 book, *Seduction of the Innocent*, was based on his study of children and comics. Although the book failed to provide the statistics of his study, Dr. Wertham's words had the desired effect. Soon, many parents forbade their children from buying or reading comic books. The U.S. Senate held an investigation about comic book censorship. Comic book sales fell dramatically. Two-thirds

*Many groups held comic book burnings to show
their disapproval of the books' content.*

of the comic books were no longer on the market.
Several comic book publishers went out of business.

Atlas Comics dropped many of its mystery and
horror books. It switched its focus to funny animal
stories, basic science fiction, and Westerns. The
company had been publishing about 80 titles a
month—now it was only publishing 12.

Black Rider

The favorite among the Old West heroes created by Lee was Black Rider. Black Rider was a peaceful doctor in a western town. But when villains came in, he would change his identity by donning a black mask, black suit, and black cape.

On one occasion, Lee decided to use a photo rather than a drawing of Black Rider on the cover of the comic book. In a black outfit and mask, Lee posed as the western hero.

Horrible Job

With the dramatic decrease in comic sales, Goodman told Lee to fire the Atlas staff. Lee dreaded this and balked at the responsibility, but he had no choice. He was forced to put many of his friends out of work.

When the government suggested a regulated censorship of comic books, comic book publishers banded together. They wanted to regulate themselves rather than have the government regulate them. With this goal in mind, they created the Comics Magazine Association of America, which formed the Comics Code Authority. The group was responsible for inspecting each comic book for what was deemed to be excessive violence or inappropriate material for young readers. Atlas Comics had fewer problems with the Comics Code Authority than other publishers. Some publishers glorified their villains, which comic critics argued encouraged children to act in criminal ways. But the majority of Lee's stories encouraged readers to identify with main characters who had honorable morals.

The entire experience changed Lee and his views of his profession. Atlas had gone from one of the largest comic book publishers in the country to one of the smallest. Only Lee, a few freelance writers, and artists Jack Kirby (who had returned to Atlas in the 1950s), and Steve Ditko remained.

By that time, Atlas was publishing comic book titles such as *Amazing Adventures* and *Strange Tales*. Both featured weird aliens such as Fin Fang Foom, a huge dragon that wore purple boxer shorts. Lee was no longer proud of the company for which he worked. He began to question everything. But just as Lee reached the depths of despair, he rose up to create *The Fantastic Four* with

Silver Age of Comics

The period from 1956 to the early 1970s was known as the Silver Age of Comics. Superhero comics had become popular again. Brand new superheroes and superhero teams were created. These new characters were the result of a new demand in the comic book market.

DC Comics began to reintroduce some of its old comic book characters from the 1940s. These included the Flash, Green Lantern, the Atom, and Hawkman. Atlas Comics, newly renamed Marvel Comics in 1963, followed DC's success during this period by introducing new characters such as Spider-Man and Daredevil, and superhero teams such as the Fantastic Four, the X-Men, and the Avengers.

Jack Kirby. Like superheroes of the comic book industry, Lee and Kirby had saved the day. By the late 1950s, superheroes had made a glorious return. ⟶

New York City Magistrate Charles F. Murphy was named administrator of the Comics Code Authority.

In the late 1950s, Lee's comic creations gained popularity.

SOARING TO GREAT HEIGHTS

Atlas Publisher Martin Goodman had stumbled across a gold mine. In May 1962, the comic books featuring the Fantastic Four, created by Stan Lee and Jack Kirby, were flying off newsstands. Goodman could not wait to see what would emerge next from Lee's creative mind. What group of superheroes would follow the Fantastic Four? Lee had a surprise for him. There would be no group. The next series Lee was to offer would spotlight one superhero—the Incredible Hulk.

The story of the Hulk resembled that of Dr. Jekyll and Mr. Hyde, the famed character created by nineteenth-century author Robert Louis Stevenson. Dr. Jekyll drank a potion to become the evil Mr. Hyde. The Hulk changed from a mild-mannered doctor named Bruce Banner into a raging monster due to poisoning by gamma rays.

After Lee came up with the Hulk, he shared his idea with Kirby. Lee remembers feeling odd about his request to Kirby. He recalled,

> *I remember telling [Kirby], "Jack, you're going to think I'm crazy, but can you draw a good-looking monster?" . . . Even as I said it, I could hear how idiotic the words must have sounded.*[1]

But Kirby came up with a monster that fit Stan's vision perfectly. And, *The Incredible Hulk* appealed to comic book readers.

Name Changes

Marvel Comics went through several different names before becoming Marvel Comics. When the company was founded in 1939 it was called Timely Comics. By the 1950s it had changed its name to Atlas Comics. Finally, the company changed to its current name, Marvel Comics, in 1963.

Along Came a Spider

Lee experienced one success after another with his philosophy of creating superheroes with human identities and real problems. But one of his greatest creations was yet to come.

One day in his office, Lee was curiously watching a fly. He marveled at how it stuck on the wall. It popped into his mind to create a superhero that could latch onto walls and ceilings. Spider-Man was born.

By 1962, Lee had created a teenager named Peter Parker to be his sticky new superhero. Parker shared the same problems many teenagers face, such as shyness and pimples. Lee deemed that Spider-Man would also be an orphan and a bit of a nerd. But Goodman hated the idea. Lee can still remember Goodman's reaction,

Comic Fans in College

During the 1960s, Marvel comic books became increasingly popular with college students. Many students related to some of the real-life issues that the superheroes faced, such as money problems. These students also embraced Stan Lee for his work with Marvel. Before long, Lee was giving lectures at universities around the country.

Lee created Spider-Man in 1962.

He said I was crazy. He said people hate spiders. He said "You want him to be a teenager? Teenagers can only be sidekicks. And you want him to have problems?" I told him I wanted [Spider-Man] to worry about money and pimples.[2]

Lee had hoped for a far more positive reaction from Goodman, but he pushed ahead anyway. Lee needed an artist who could bring Spider-Man to life. First, he took the Spider-Man concept to illustrator Jack Kirby. Kirby sketched his idea of what the character should look like. Lee, however, thought Kirby's Spider-Man appeared too big and muscular. Kirby told Lee to feel free to take Spider-Man to another artist. Lee turned to artist Steve Ditko. The Spider-Man Ditko created looked more like an average guy. This depiction fit Lee's idea of the character perfectly. Lee placed Spider-Man on the cover of the final issue of *Amazing Fantasy*. Three months later, the sales figures showed that Spider-Man was a huge hit.

Goodman quickly changed his mind about Spider-Man. He told Lee to turn the comic into a series. Lee created colorful villains for Spider-Man to battle, such as Green Goblin and Dr. Octopus. By 1962, the circulation of Atlas comic books had grown from 7 million to 13 million in just one year.

Thor and More

Following the creation of the Fantastic Four, Hulk, and Spider-Man, what was next for Stan Lee? After giving it some thought, Lee figured that his next superhero should feature super strength. He created Thor—the Norse God of Thunder.

Lee believed by making Thor a god, the character could boast greater strength than any human superhero. But most people had only heard about Greek gods or Roman gods. Lee was inspired by the imagery of a Norse god that looked like a Viking of the eleventh century with a long, flowing beard, a horned helmet, and a wooden club. However, Lee's Thor did not have a beard, and he carried a magic hammer rather than a club. Thor also had the ability to fly.

Once again, Lee was on a roll. His creative

The Mysterious Artist

The world certainly got to know the most famous comic book character drawn by Steve Ditko. But few people ever got to know Ditko himself. The *Spider-Man* illustrator was a very withdrawn person. Ditko became one of Stan Lee's favorite freelance artists in the 1960s. Lee could always depend on Ditko when he needed work done quickly. They developed a strong and fruitful business relationship. "He was a joy and a pleasure to work with," Lee said.[3]

However, Ditko never opened up to the outside world. Despite the tremendous success of *Spider-Man*, he has declined interviews with the media or even to have his picture taken since the 1960s. His life has been a mystery, which is the way he apparently prefers it. Ditko did agree to an interview in 1968, and said,

> When I do a job, it's not my personality that I'm offering the readers, but my [artwork]. It's not what I'm like that counts, it is what I did and how well it was done. I produce a product, a comic art story. Steve Ditko is the brand name.[4]

Ditko is still credited as the cocreator of *Spider-Man* since he was the one who brought the main character to life.

The Silver Surfer

One Marvel character that did not find its audience was the Silver Surfer. Jack Kirby had created the Silver Surfer as a side character for *The Fantastic Four*, but Lee decided to give him his own comic book. The character was trapped on Earth, but he really wanted to return to his home planet. His evil master, Galactus, prevented him from coming back.

Unfortunately for Lee, *The Silver Surfer* did not sell well because it was geared toward an older audience and was offered at a higher price than the other Marvel comic books.

juices flowed when he created Iron Man, who had been Tony Stark, a billionaire weapons manufacturer. Stark had been captured by an enemy during a war and was told the only way he could be released was if he created a weapon for them. Instead, Stark used the material to build an iron suit for himself, thus becoming Iron Man. To make the story a bit more dramatic, Lee wrote that Iron Man had been shot by the enemy and had a piece of shrapnel lodged near his heart. Even the slightest movement could kill him. Lee's Iron Man became immensely popular. Comic books featuring characters such as Sergeant Fury and his Howling Commandos and Dr. Strange also brought success.

Time for a Team

In 1963, the same year that Atlas Comics was renamed Marvel Comics, Lee felt that it was time to bring another team of superheroes into the comic book world. He created a group whose superpowers did not emerge until they became teenagers. He named the group the X-Men. They were not all men, however. Marvel Girl, who had the power to move things without touching them, was also part of the X-Men.

With the tremendous popularity of the X-Men, Lee decided to create another team. Current Marvel characters Hulk, Thor, Iron Man, Ant Man, and the Wasp became the Avengers. Even the Fantastic Four made a guest appearance in the first issue. And all for 12 cents, which was the cost of a Marvel comic book in the early 1960s.

Lee remembers this time very fondly. He said,

[It] was an era I'll never forget. [It was] a time of cascading creativity and escalating excitement . . . . I felt as though everything

Daredevil

During the 1960s, Lee created the first blind superhero. Matt Murdock was the typical teenager who transformed into Daredevil. Murdock was blinded when radioactive waste was poured into his eyes as he was trying to save someone's life. Although the character lost his sight, he gained super strength in all his other senses, such as taste and smell.

Lee was concerned about the reaction to Daredevil by blind people and organizations that help the blind. He was thrilled when he received letters thanking him for creating a blind super-hero.

was going perfectly. There was no reason to worry or be concerned about the company . . . . Our future was assured. We just had to keep doing what we were doing and the future would take care of itself.[5]

In 1963, the first issue of The X-Men comic book arrived at newsstands.

Jack Kirby illustrated many comics for Lee, including The Fantastic Four.

The Marvel Age

Lee had created a large number of superheroes. He had also placed all his superheroes in New York City. Lee was born and raised there, so he knew it well. He would use New York landmarks in his stories. Eventually he decided to play games of mix and match. He would write scripts in which a *Fantastic Four* character such as the Human Torch would meet Spider-Man while searching for the Hulk on the streets of New York. He had created the Marvel Universe.

Lee also started what became known as the Marvel Method, which began when Lee gave his artists a general idea of a story, its characters, and the plot. He allowed the artists to bring the work to life. He then would add the dialogue and captions. This system, which nearly every comic book publisher has adopted, allowed Lee to keep all his artists working on projects at the same time. Eventually Ditko and other artists would create plots themselves, which saved time for the busy Lee.

The Marvel Method also resulted in well-illustrated comics. Because the artists did not have the dialogue in the place yet, they used the drawings to create the story. This often resulted in characters with more detailed facial expression and body movements. Unfortunately, the Marvel Method caused some

Double Duty

Decades earlier, some of the Timely artists, including Jack Kirby, did work on the side for DC Comics. Now in the mid-1960s, several DC illustrators brought characters and stories to life by freelancing for Marvel. The artists, of course, wanted to avoid being caught by DC, by which they were still employed. Therefore, they all used pseudonyms or false names.

problems between Lee and the Marvel artists. Artists such as Kirby and Ditko often created whole stories for a comic book. Kirby claimed that he created stories without any input from Lee at all. But it was usually Lee who got the credit for the story.

The artists grew frustrated with the attention Lee was getting for their work.

CREATING COMMUNITY

Although Lee is known for creating some of Marvel's most famous characters, he is perhaps more famous for establishing a community of Marvel Comics readers. Lee was interested in

---

Diversity in Comics

Lee decided in the early 1960s that his comic books should show the diversity of the American population. So when creating *Sergeant Nick Fury and His Howling Commandos*, he gave the lead character an ethnically and racially mixed platoon in World War II. Included in the group were Jewish Izzy Cohen, Italian Dino Manelli, Irish Dum-Dum Dugan, and African-American Gabriel Jones.

Lee was warned that there were still many prejudiced people throughout the country and that such an idea might not work. Marvel publisher Martin Goodman told Lee that conjuring up World War II stories in the 1960s would not work. Another problem was the title *Sgt. Fury and His Howling Commandos*—it was so long, it barely fit across the top of the comic book.

But with the artistic talents of Jack Kirby, the comic books featuring Nick Fury and his diverse group of friends became an immediate best seller. Marvel published it for several years before dropping it. But readers demanded that Nick Fury return, so the old issues were reprinted and sold almost as well as the original ones.

creating a sense of community among Marvel fans because he knew it would result in more comic book sales. In one successful attempt to develop a relationship with Marvel fans, Lee began a "Letters to the Editor" column. Readers could write in to express their opinions about any of the comic books or characters. Lee would print selected letters and his replies. He tried to make his responses humorous and informal because he wanted to make all his comic books reader-friendly.

Lee also ran contests to create more interest among the current readers and lure in new readers. In January 1965, Marvel had announced it was starting a club for its readers. Its initials would be MMMS. Readers who figured out what the initials stood for were given prizes. Marvel dropped hints in its various issues before finally revealing that it stood for the Merry Marvel Marching Society. But the MMMS only lasted for a few years. According to Lee,

Excelsior

One of Lee's favorite words is "excelsior." It is a word that was used centuries ago meaning upward and onward to greater glory. Lee liked the way it sounded, and he appreciated what it meant as a philosophy for Marvel Comics. In the early 1960s, Lee began including the word "excelsior" by his signature whenever he signed his name.

Goodman claimed the club was too expensive to maintain.

A few years later, Lee formed another fan club called Friends of ol' Marvel (FOOM). It quickly gained thousands of members, but Lee was told to disband that one as well because it was not making a large profit.

Stan's Soapbox

One of several ways Lee had of opening communication with his readers in the early 1960s was a column called "Stan's Soapbox." He used this column to write about anything he liked and invited responses from the readers. Lee wrote in his biography about the column, "I'd write little messages like, 'Hey, I hope you enjoyed this month's Hulk. Didja know it was drawn by Herb Trimpe, whose skin seems to be turning green the more he draws our jolly green giant?' . . . Basically, I wanted to give our fans personal stuff, make them feel they were a part of Marvel."[1]

PRESSURES AND DIFFICULTIES

Despite his successes, Lee was heading for difficult times. He began to feel overwhelmed by his numerous duties at work. He was not only Marvel's editor-in-chief and art director, he was still writing stories for most of the comics.

In addition, relations became strained between Lee and artists such as Ditko and Kirby. Lee's heavy workload forced him to give Ditko the responsibility of creating the *Spider-Man* story lines, but the two argued frequently about the direction Ditko was taking the superhero. It reached a point where Lee and Ditko were not

Lee believed that creating clubs like MMMS helped sell more comic books.

speaking to each other. Ditko solved that problem when he quit Marvel Comics in 1966. Lee later wished Kirby and Ditko had expressed their feelings to him.

Meanwhile, tragedy struck in Lee's personal life. One day his brother Larry called and said in

Green Goblin Twist

One disagreement that might have played a role in Steve Ditko quitting Marvel in 1966 centered on *Spider-Man* villain Green Goblin. In one issue, Lee wrote about the unmasking of the Goblin. Lee argued that when the Goblin's face was revealed, it should be someone the readers already knew. Ditko wanted it to be someone that the readers had not seen before. In a dramatic twist, the Green Goblin was unmasked and revealed to be Norman Osborn. Norman was the father of Peter Parker's friend, Harry Osborn, and a character that the readers already knew.

a trembling voice that their father Jack had died unexpectedly. Lee felt emptiness in his life. He had always looked forward to visits from his father. Lee and his family then sold their New Jersey home and moved back to New York City.

While Lee moved his family, Marvel continued to move in a positive direction. Not only was it selling an estimated 50 million comic books a year by the mid-1960s, but its work had also expanded into animated television. *The Marvel Super Heroes* show debuted in 1966.

Marvel was still a shining star. However, little did Lee know, everything was about to change again at Marvel. And it eventually challenged Lee in a way he had never been challenged before.

Stan Lee helped to create Marvel's strong fan base.

Stan Lee wrote and produced many comic books for Marvel Comics.

UNHAPPY PROMOTION

By the mid-1960s, Stan Lee had become very successful in the comic book industry. It seemed everything he touched turned to gold. And Marvel was at the top of its game. Although DC Comics had established a market for superhero magazines decades earlier, DC was now following the trends set by Marvel. DC and other publishers were scrambling to create bold covers and strange creatures for its comic books in an attempt to match Marvel in popularity.

Lee had revolutionized the comic book industry by writing not only for kids, but for adults as well. In a 1968 interview he said,

> *Our goal is that someday an intelligent adult would not be embarrassed to walk down the street with a comic magazine. I don't know whether we can ever bring this off, but it's something to shoot for.*[1]

The Perfect Film and Chemical Corporation had been looking for a story to develop into a film for fall 1968. It wanted to buy Marvel Comics from Martin Goodman. Lee believed the purchase would keep Marvel on solid financial ground for years. What he did not realize was

Popular in Mexico

The most unusual public event Lee attended was in Mexico City. He did not realize how popular he was in Mexico until he noticed the six bodyguards in attendance. The authorities thought fans would mob him. They were right. Approximately 15,000 people showed up. Lee recalled the visit, "As I was walking through with three big [bodyguards] on each side of me, people kept yelling, 'Olé! Olé! Stan Lee! Stan Lee!'. . . . It was unbelievable. I'll never forget it. One of the guards said, 'Stan, I swear, you could run for president [of Mexico] and you'd be elected right here and now.'"[2]

that this move and others would hurt the company and the relationships of the people who worked for it. Perfect Film, which soon changed its name to Cadence Industries, offered an estimated $15 million for Marvel. Goodman was told that the sale would only go through if Lee remained on board.

Jim Warren

In the early 1970s, Lee became influenced by the work of the Warren Publishing Company and its publisher, Jim Warren. The company produced black-and-white horror comic books such as *Creepy, Eerie,* and *Vampirella.* Those works motivated Lee to get Marvel involved in creating horror books as well.

Lee was flattered that such a large corporation thought that highly of him. A friend told him that he could hold out for as much money as he wanted since Goodman desperately needed to sign him to a new contract for the deal to go through. But Lee was not motivated by money. He took Goodman's first offer without a written agreement.

It was a mistake. Goodman promised other valuable assets to go along with the raise in salary, but Lee claimed to have never received them. And, he could not do anything about it because he never got it in writing.

Lee was left with a raise and nothing else. Upset over the broken promise from Goodman, Lee strongly considered quitting.

NEW JOB, NEW RESPONSIBILITIES

The people at Cadence understood the value of Lee's creativity, relationship with the readers, and genius for promotion. Lee was offered the position of publisher, which he gladly accepted. He turned the creative responsibilities over to others. For the first time in his career, he stopped writing. Meanwhile, ideas for promoting Marvel began filtering through his mind. He knew its comic books had millions of faithful fans, but he also understood that millions of others had never heard of Marvel or were simply more attracted to its rivals.

Lee soon became very familiar with plane travel. His job had him

A New Editor

After Lee became publisher, he needed to find a new editor-in-chief for Marvel Comics. He quickly decided on Roy Thomas. Thomas had been lured away from DC Comics in 1965. He was considered one of the top writers in the comic book industry. He may have been the most important addition to the Marvel creative team in that era.

touring the country to promote Marvel. He spoke at hundreds of colleges and universities. Lee did not limit his lecture tours to the United States. His tours included stops in Japan, Italy, Germany, Poland, Denmark, France, Spain, and Portugal. Lee knew that it was not just children reading comic books anymore. Even the most intelligent college students had become avid fans. All of the publicity resulted in Lee becoming a cultural icon. He enjoyed it when the media began referring to him as "Mr. Marvel."

Yet all was not well with Marvel or with the comic book industry. In the late 1960s, the price of comic books increased

Dress Down, Dress Up

Stan Lee never considered himself fashionable. So he was in for a rude awakening when he began his college lecture tours in the late 1960s. His first speech was at Bard College in New York. He was so thrilled at the invitation that he dressed up in his best suit and tie. But young people during that era did not dress up often. They showed up wearing beards, torn undershirts, and raggedy jeans. Fortunately, all went well. Lee was received with enthusiasm and asked to stay for dinner. But he vowed he would not make the same fashion mistake again.

His next invitation was to Princeton University in New Jersey. Recalling the way the students were dressed at Bard, Lee put on his oldest jeans, faded shirt, and tennis shoes. But he was stunned when he walked in to see the students dressed impeccably with suits and ties. Lee, however, was again lucky. Both the students and teachers responded to his speech enthusiastically and made him an honorary member of the school's debating club.

from 12 cents to 15 cents. This
change hurt circulation. Marvel titles
such as *The Silver Surfer* and *Sergeant
Nick Fury* were discontinued. Even *The
Incredible Hulk* and *Captain America Comics*
struggled to make money.

More Changes

By the early 1970s, readers
were once again losing interest in
superheroes. The United States was
fighting in the Vietnam War. The
public was in conflict over the U.S.
involvement in the war. The comic
book industry moved in a serious
direction.

In 1970, DC Comics writer
Dennis O'Neil and artist Neal Adams
had superheroes Green Lantern
and Green Arrow fighting racism
and poverty. Marvel answered by
creating its own stories that dealt
with serious issues. One *Spider–Man*
story line had Peter Parker's best
friend Harry Osborn suffering from

The Death of Gwen Stacy

Many of Marvel's comics took on a serious tone in the early 1970s. One example of this occurred in the *Spider-Man* comics. Stan wrote an issue entitled *The Night Gwen Stacey Died.* In this issue, Peter Parker's girlfriend, Gwen Stacey, was killed in a battle with Spider-Man's enemy Green Goblin. Spider-Man was unable to save her.

This event had a large impact on Spider-Man fans. In the past, Spider-Man very seldom failed to save a loved one. This instance reflected the darker tone present in comics during this time period.

Stan Lee often worked with artist John Romita, right.

drug addiction. The world was changing and Lee
wanted Marvel to change along with it. But stories of
superheroes now seemed irrelevant to many readers.
The *Spider-Man* comic books were selling 370,000

copies a month in 1968. Four years later, that had dropped to 290,000. To make matters worse, Jack Kirby quit Marvel in March 1970. But Lee was fortunate. Most comic book publishers had gone out of business by the early 1970s. Marvel was one of just six that remained.

The ever-changing tastes of comic book readers forced another change in the 1970s. Horror titles became popular again. Marvel released titles such as *Tomb of Dracula, Man-Thing, Werewolf by Night, Chamber of Chills,* and *Dead of Night.*

Early that decade, Marvel pursued a plan that would prove disastrous. In an attempt to surpass DC Comics in the battle for readership, Marvel rapidly expanded its output. Its number of titles skyrocketed from about 12 in 1970 to 50 in 1975. For a while, it added one new comic book a month. It was believed that Marvel could overwhelm DC by sheer numbers. The strategy failed. Too much activity resulted in confusion. In an attempt to cut costs, the number of pages were reduced in each comic book. Meanwhile, the quality of the work suffered. Disenchanted readers cancelled their subscriptions, which led to cuts in salaries. The writers and illustrators at Marvel became unhappy.

Everything was going wrong, and Lee hated his job as publisher. He missed the creative aspect of working in the comic book world. Fortunately, Marvel and its characters were popular enough for executives in the newspaper, television, and movie industries to crave a piece of the Marvel Universe.

When Marvel comics such as Spider-Man were turned into movies,
Lee was invited to attend their premieres.

Lee and Nicholas Hammond, actor from The Amazing Spider-Man *television series, talked in 1978.*

BRANCHING OUT

The blossoming of Marvel Comics into the mainstream American media began in the late 1970s. Lee was asked if he would reformat some of his characters into newspaper comic strips. Lee was not initially thrilled about that possibility.

He understood that comic book stories are developed across 20 or more pages. Newspaper strips are limited to five or six panels. That did not give the writer much of an opportunity to tell a story every day. Lee turned down the offer, but he remained intrigued at the notion of his company being represented in newspapers throughout the world.

Soon, Denny Allen contacted Lee. Allen was president of the Register and Tribune Syndicate, which placed new comic strips into newspapers. Allen was interested in a Spider-Man strip that would appear in newspapers seven days a week. He even gave Lee the freedom to have them written any way he pleased. In January 1977, *Spider-Man* the comic strip was created with Marvel's John Romita handling the artistic chores. The comic strip was a major success and appeared in more than 200 newspapers worldwide. Eventually, Lee took

Jim Galton

One of the most successful hires at Marvel Comics occurred in 1975 when Jim Galton became the new president of the company. Galton and Lee forged a relationship in which Galton took care of all the business, which allowed Lee to concentrate on his creative projects that would expand the Marvel Universe.

A Replacement for the Human Torch

When producers put together the cast for NBC's new TV series *The Fantastic Four,* they replaced the Human Torch with a new character named H.E.R.B.I.E., which stood for Humanoid Experimental Robot B-Type Integrated Electronics. He was a robot built by Mr. Fantastic.

There was a rumor that the producers created a new character rather than use the Human Torch because they thought that the Human Torch would lead children to set themselves on fire. However, the real reason the producers created a new character was because another company had already purchased the right to use the Human Torch.

over the writing and his brother, Larry, became responsible for the illustrations. A year later, Spider-Man was turned into a live television show called *The Amazing Spider-Man.* Actor Nicholas Hammond played the part of Spider-Man and Peter Parker.

Also in 1978, Lee reunited with Jack Kirby to create a book-length version of *The Silver Surfer.* This suggested that there was less friction between them than many believed when Kirby left Marvel in 1970. Lee was thrilled that a friend and associate for so many years felt close enough to him to collaborate on a project.

"Fantastic" on TV

Spider-Man was not the only one to make it onto the television screen. In 1978, NBC began showing an animated television show of *The Fantastic Four.* Lee and Roy Thomas, who had quit as editor-in-chief to pursue his passion for writing, combined to create some of the scripts. But a far more famous program based on a Marvel character featuring live actors would soon appear on CBS. It was *The Incredible Hulk*.

The television series starred veteran actor Bill Bixby as Dr. Banner, the tortured soul who was transformed into the Hulk when he was angered. Bodybuilder Lou Ferrigno played the Hulk. Ferrigno appeared for only about five minutes in each one-hour program and never spoke in that role. But *The Incredible Hulk* was a surprise hit as the first live-action show featuring a Marvel character.

The emergence of comic book stores also helped

Sealed with a KISS

The most unusual publicity stunt the people at Marvel dreamed up during Stan Lee's time as publisher centered on the rock group KISS. The members of KISS, who covered their faces with makeup, were immensely popular in the late 1970s. So Marvel planned to launch a KISS comic book.

The band was flown to Buffalo, New York, where the Marvel books were printed. They were to be escorted to a vat filled with red ink. Each of them was to prick their finger with a pin, then allow a few drops of their blood to drip into the vat of red ink. Marvel would then claim that actual KISS blood went into the printing of every one of their comic books.

Lee flew with the group to Buffalo. When the plane landed, they were met by a limousine. Police motorcycles with flashing lights escorted the limousine through Buffalo, stopping traffic along the way. Lee admitted that he felt guilty that people driving along the streets of Buffalo had to stop just so kids in a rock group could drop their blood into a vat of red ink!

In the 1970s, comic book stores helped Marvel sell more comics.

bring the comic book industry back to life. In neighborhoods throughout the country, new stores opened that specialized in comic books. This market not only catered to those who looked to keep up with their current comic book characters, but also to a new type of consumer. These were the collectors who bought and sold vintage comic books, some from decades past, for their value. The most popular old comic books in excellent condition could sell for hundreds and even thousands of dollars. Comic book stores soon became a place for comic book fans to hang around and discuss comic books. This helped to strengthen the community aspect of comic books.

Though Lee and the entire industry benefited greatly from that new direction and marketing of comic books, he was spending an increasing amount of time in Los Angeles. During the late 1970s, he worked to develop films in which Marvel characters would appear and sought to create comic books based on Hollywood films.

One such project revolved around the wildly popular movie *Star Wars*. In 1977, Lee secured a contract that allowed Marvel to publish a six-episode series of comic books based on that film. The series sold more than 1 million copies. Marvel was overwhelmed with requests to keep up with demand.

HOLLYWOOD, HERE HE COMES

The potential for comic book characters as film stars was realized in 1978. *Superman: The Movie* grossed $300 million worldwide. Its popularity proved quite remarkable considering the DC comic books featuring Superman were selling poorly at that time.

In 1980, Lee became the creative director of Marvel Productions in Hollywood. He and his wife, Joan, moved to Los Angeles. As he wrote in his autobiography, this move had been his dream for quite a while:

> *In the past, whenever I visited Los Angeles, I felt as though I had come to Nirvana. The indescribably beautiful weather, the mind-boggling scenery with mountains in the background and the ocean a stone's throw away . . . trees, gardens and flowers everywhere, and most exiting of all, the ability to drive a convertible with the top down [12] months a year. I wanted it. I wanted to live in L.A.*[1]

Lee continued to dive into his work with enthusiasm in Los Angeles. He was always looking for ways to expand Marvel Comics. By 1982, he was engaged in several projects

Joan Gets Creative

The creative bug bit Lee's wife Joan after the couple moved to Los Angeles. Joan decided she wanted to write a fiction book. Lee was skeptical because she had never written anything before. But the book, which was titled *The Pleasure Palace,* was published in 1987.

involving Marvel characters. These included live-action television shows featuring Daredevil and the Black Widow, movies involving Captain America and Howard the Duck, and Broadway plays spotlighting Thor and Captain America. Many of Lee's projects, however, never came to fruition or failed to capture the imagination of American audiences. *Howard the Duck*, which was based on a Marvel comic book, and *Captain America* did not fare well at the box office. Some fans believed that Lee had simply pushed Marvel stories and characters into places they could not succeed—all in hopes of gaining more media attention for Marvel. But Lee blamed poor production for the failure of those two movies. He believed the small budgets of the filmmakers doomed both.

But this was not the end of Marvel movies. Marvel and Stan Lee still had success ahead of them. One Marvel

David DePatie

When Lee became creative head of Marvel Productions, David DePatie was hired to run the new animation studio. DePatie had served as a producer at Warner Brothers, which featured such animated stars as Bugs Bunny and Daffy Duck. He also helped produce the Pink Panther cartoons in the late 1960s and early 1970s.

character in particular was about to become the most
successful movie superhero the world had ever seen.

Lee became creative director of Marvel Productions in Hollywood.

Spider-Man 2 *starred Tobey Maguire,* right, *and Kirsten Dunst,* middle.
Avi Arad, left, *produced the film.*

Takeover and a
Smash Hit

*I*n the 1980s, Marvel Comics was bought
and sold twice in two years. In 1986, just
as it was celebrating its twenty-fifth anniversary as
Marvel Comics, it was purchased by New World
Entertainment. In 1988, a group led by a wealthy

man named Ron Perelman bought New World and organized a new company called Marvel Films. Lee was selected to lead that operation.

Lee was never particularly interested in corporate dealings. His experience as Marvel publisher further soured him on working on the business side of his professional world. But when Lee met with Bill Bevins, who would lead things at Marvel for Perelman, he came away smiling and a little confused.

At the meeting, Bevins almost immediately asked Lee what his annual salary at Marvel was. Then Bevins told him that he would now be earning nearly triple his old salary. Lee recalled his surprise,

> *At first I wasn't sure if I had heard him correctly, but was reluctant to ask him to repeat what he had said, in case he'd change his mind. When I got home and told Joanie what had transpired, we spent quite a while trying to figure out*

Jack Kirby's Funeral

When leaving Marvel in 1970, Kirby expressed his view that he was more responsible than Lee for the company's success. When Kirby died, some believed the family had remembered the fallout between the two and would keep Lee away from the funeral.

However, Lee did attend Kirby's funeral. He sat in the back in an attempt to keep people from approaching him about his relationship with Kirby. Lee later spoke with Kirby's wife, Roz, and the issue was smoothed over.

what he must have really said —what could have sounded like
"triple"? We couldn't think of anything so we decided to wait
until pay day and see what the actual payment would be.[1]

Lee discovered when the check came that his
salary had indeed been almost tripled. But not all was
well with Marvel and the comic book industry when
the bottom fell out of the collector market.

Speculators and the Comics Glut

The beginning of the end occurred in the 1990s,
when publishers began printing millions of extra
comic books to satisfy readers who were now also
comic book speculators. Speculators buy comics
believing that the publications will be valuable to sell
in the future. In the late 1990s, when the speculators
tried to sell their comic books, they discovered there
was no market for them. People only wanted to buy
rare comic books.

The result was that the publishers had spent too
much money printing too many comic books. Supply
greatly outweighed demand. Readers were no longer
buying comic books they could not sell. And the
owners of comic book stores could no longer pay for
the ones they ordered. Many went out of business.

Marvel lost money on its comic books and other ventures. Once again, it fell into new ownership in which all employee contracts would be terminated and new ones drawn up. Lee was told that his contract would be reduced to just two years and his salary cut in half. But he hired a lawyer who negotiated a new deal that restored Lee's pay to its previous level and allowed him to work on outside projects.

Lee was now in his mid-seventies. He no longer worked exclusively for Marvel. But he continued to work on bringing Spider-Man to the silver screen. Cannon Films had acquired the film rights to the *Spider-*

Over the Great Wall

Stan Lee has traveled to many different countries to speak. But he flew farther than ever before to address an audience in 2000. That was the year he was invited to China. Lee was one of the few people in the entertainment industry to ever speak in the huge Asian country. He spoke at the Great Hall of the People in Beijing.

Lee was surprised to learn that the popularity of Marvel comic book characters had reached the second-most populous country in the world. He was interviewed by a reporter from the *People's Daily* newspaper about *Spider-Man*. Lee promised to send the writer several autographed copies of *Spider-Man* comic books when he returned to the United States. He was particularly thrilled that *Spider-Man* remained popular, especially so far away, when many believed the character had reached its peak in popularity in the 1960s and 1970s.

While in Beijing, Lee was inducted into the Japan-China Digital Manga Association as an honorary member. This association is an animation trade group, and Lee was the first Western artist to be so honored.

Man Comics in 1985. Eight different movie scripts were turned in, including one in which Peter Parker was transformed into a giant eight-legged tarantula. But Cannon fell into financial ruin, leaving Spider-Man as a free agent again. Other movie studios battled for the rights to turn Spider-Man into a film star, and finally in 1999, Columbia Pictures won.

Because of the contract he signed in 1998, Lee was no longer considered the head of Marvel Studios. Avi Arad now held that position and negotiated the deals that brought *X-Men*, *Spider-Man*, *Daredevil*, *Fantastic Four*, and *The Hulk* to theaters after the turn of the century. Lee had been working on only promotion and creating the *Spider-Man* newspaper comic strip. He was listed in the credits as executive producer and received a share of the profits from the movies.

In the Movies

A small part has been written in for Lee in many of the movies featuring Marvel characters. Lee played a hot dog vendor in *X-Men*, a mailman who greets the heroes in *Fantastic Four*, a guest at a party in *Iron Man*, and a citizen who accidentally swallows a drink mixed with Bruce Banner's blood in *The Incredible Hulk*. He has been provided cameo appearances in several other films as well.

MORE AND MORE MOVIES

Although Lee had planted the seeds for the film successes of Marvel characters, he received little credit for them. In 2000, *X-Men* became the first successful Marvel Comic movie. The film earned $157 million. Around this time Lee stated,

> I take great pleasure in the successes at Marvel. But I can't claim to be responsible for all of them right now. The only responsibility I can perhaps claim is that I was the cocreator of so many of these characters.[2]

But *X-Men* was only the beginning. *Spider-Man* became the highest-grossing film of 2002 in the United States, earning more than $400 million. More Marvel movies followed. Some of the most popular movies were two sequels to *Spider-Man*, two sequels to *X-Men*, two Fantastic Four movies, and *Iron Man*.

Marvel Movies

- *Howard the Duck* (1986)
- *Captain America* (1990)
- *Blade* (1998)
- *X-Men* (2000)
- *Blade II* (2002)
- *Spider-Man* (2002)
- *Daredevil* (2003)
- *Hulk* (2003)
- *X2: X-Men United* (2003)
- *Blade: Trinity* (2004)
- *Spider-Man 2* (2004)
- *The Punisher* (2004)
- *Elektra* (2005)
- *Man-Thing* (2005)
- *Fantastic Four* (2005)
- *X-Men: The Last Stand* (2006)
- *Ghost Rider* (2007)
- *Fantastic Four: Rise of the Silver Surfer* (2007)
- *Spider-Man 3* (2007)
- *Iron Man* (2008)
- *The Incredible Hulk* (2008)
- *Punisher: War Zone* (2008)
- *X-Men Origins: Wolverine* (2009)

Stan Lee starred in Who Wants to Be a Superhero?, *a reality television show.*

Iron Man earned about $580 million worldwide, followed by *Fantastic Four* at about $330 million. Sequels to *Spider-Man*, *X-Men*, and *Fantastic Four* each earned more than $290 million.

ADDING TO HIS LEGACY

In late 2001, Lee helped form a new company called POW!, which stands for Purveyors of Wonder.

The company develops films, television shows, published materials, and games. He also starred in a popular reality television show called *Who Wants to Be a Superhero?* that aired for two seasons on the Sci Fi channel.

Lee and Marvel had all but parted ways, but the last thing that he would ever do was retire. Instead, Lee rewrote a chapter from his past when he returned to political humor. During the 2008 U.S. presidential campaign, he released a book titled *Election Daze* in which he inserted funny, phony dialogue to photos of candidates.

In 2008, Lee was presented with the National Medal of Arts for his immense achievements. Decades after producing his first successful comic books, Lee's creations continue to be successful. The characters he created can now be enjoyed through a variety of different media such as movies, television, novels, and of course,

Famous Friends

Lee's growing popularity over the years brought him in contact with many famous people. Among those were actor Tony Curtis, boxing champion Muhammad Ali, presidents George W. Bush, Bill Clinton, and Ronald Reagan, and Gray Davis, the governor of California. Lee also met Tom Bradley, the mayor of Los Angeles, when Bradley presented him with the Certificate of Appreciation.

comic books. Stan Lee will always be remembered for creating superheroes that will be enjoyed by generations to come. ⌐

President George W. Bush presented Stan Lee with
the 2008 National Medal of Arts.

TIMELINE

1922	1929	1936
Stanley Martin Lieber is born in New York City on December 28.	The Lieber family struggles financially during the Great Depression.	Lee earns prizes in The Biggest News of the Week contest, run by the *New York Herald Tribune*.

1945	1947	1953
Lee returns to Timely as its editor and chief writer.	Lee marries Joan Boocock on December 5.	Lee writes "The Raving Maniac" in defense of the comic book industry.

1940

Recently out of high school, Lee is hired by Timely Publications.

1941

In May, *Captain America #3* features Lee's first comic book script.

1942

Lee volunteers for the U.S. Army on November 9.

1960

Lee plans to quit Atlas Comics and find another writing job, but stays and creates *The Fantastic Four.*

1961

Fantastic Four #1 is published in November.

1962

The Incredible Hulk #1, created by Lee and artist Jack Kirby, is published in May.

TIMELINE

1962	1963	1966
Spider-Man debuts in *Amazing Fantasy #15* in August.	Marvel unveils Iron Man in *Tales of Suspense #39* in March.	Some of Lee's characters make television debuts in the animated *Marvel Super Heroes* show.

1981	1986	1992
Animated cartoons *Spider-Man and His Amazing Friends* and *Hulk* appear on Saturday morning television.	The first major film based on a Marvel character, *Howard the Duck*, is a flop at the box office.	The animated series *X-Men* is launched.

1972

Lee is promoted to publisher of Marvel Comics in March.

1978

The first live-action Marvel television show begins with the debut of *The Amazing Spider-Man.*

1980

The Lees move to Los Angeles, where Stan begins to market Marvel Comics projects to Hollywood.

2000

The first major movie production featuring a Marvel character debuts when *X-Men* is released in the summer.

2002

The movie *Spider-Man* is released on May 3. It earns $403 million at the theaters.

2008

Lee is honored with the National Medal of Arts.

Essential Facts

Date of Birth

December 28, 1922

Place of Birth

New York City, New York

Parents

Jack and Celia Lieber

Education

DeWitt Clinton High School, Bronx, NY; City College of New York, New York City, NY

Marriage

Joan Boocock (December 5, 1947)

Children

Joan Celia Lieber

Jan Lieber (died 1953)

CAREER HIGHLIGHTS

❖ In May 1941, Stan Lee's first piece of comic book writing titled "The Traitor's Revenge" appeared in *Captain American #3*.

❖ In 1941, Lee became temporary editorial director of Timely Comics at the age of 18.

❖ Stan Lee's comic book creations of *The Fantastic Four, The Incredible Hulk, Thor, Spider-Man,* and *The X-Men* made him a popular creator in the comic book industry during the 1960s.

❖ In 1972, Lee became publisher of Marvel Comics.

❖ In 2002, *Spider-Man* made more than $400 million at the box office.

RESIDENCES

New York City, New York; Los Angeles, California

CONFLICTS

❖ Stan Lee conflicted with artists Jack Kirby and Steve Ditko about credit for work and the direction of the plots in some comic books.

❖ Dr. Frederic Wertham's book, *Seduction of the Innocent,* contributed to a large drop in comic book sales in the early 1950s.

❖ The popularity of comic books wavered in the 1970s.

QUOTE

"Our goal is that someday an intelligent adult would not be embarrassed to walk down the street with a comic magazine. I don't know whether we can ever bring this off, but it's something to shoot for."—*Stan Lee,* 1968

ADDITIONAL RESOURCES

SELECT BIBLIOGRAPHY

Daniels, Les. *Marvel: Five Fabulous Decades of the World's Greatest Comics*. New York: Harry N. Abrams, 1993.

Lee, Stan, and George Mair. *Excelsior! The Amazing Life of Stan Lee*. New York: Simon and Schuster, 2002.

Raphael, Jordan, and Tom Spurgeon. *Stan Lee and the Rise and Fall of the American Comic Book*. Chicago, IL: Chicago Review Press, 2003.

Wright, Bradford W. *Comic Book Nation: The Transformation of Youth Culture in America*. Baltimore, MD: Johns Hopkins University Press, 2001.

FURTHER READING

McLaughlin, Jeff. *Stan Lee: Conversations*. Jackson, MS: University Press of Mississippi, 2007.

Miller, Raymond H. *Inventors and Creators: Stan Lee*. Chicago, IL: KidHaven Press, 2006.

Ronin, Ro. *Tales to Astonish*. New York: St. Martin's Press, 2005.

Wallace, Daniel, Tom Brevoort, Andrew Darling, Tom DeFalco, Peter Sanderson, and Michael Teitelbaum. *The Marvel Encyclopedia: The Complete Guide to the Characters of the Marvel Universe*. New York: DK Publishing, 2006.

WEB LINKS

To learn more about Stan Lee, visit ABDO Publishing Company online at **www.abdopublishing.com**. Web sites about Stan Lee are featured on our Book Links page. These links are routinely monitored and updated to provide the most current information available.

Places to Visit

Museum of Comic and Cartoon Art
594 Broadway Avenue, Suite 401, New York, NY, 10012
212-254-3511
www.moccany.org
This museum displays collections of all genres of comic and cartoon art, including animation, cartoons, comic books, and various types of illustration.

The Ohio State University Cartoon Research Library
27 West 17th Avenue Mall, Columbus, OH 43210
614-292-0538
cartoons.osu.edu
The library provides access to printed cartoon art from the United States, including editorial cartoons, comic strips, comic books, graphic novels, sports cartoons, and magazine cartoons.

Toonseum at the Children's Museum of Pittsburgh
10 Children's Way, Pittsburgh, PA, 15212
412-332-5058
www.toonseum.com
This museum is housed within the Children's Museum of Pittsburgh. It boasts a comic book section and is geared toward those interested in cartooning, animation, and drawing.

GLOSSARY

animated
Moving illustrations.

art director
A person in charge of the artistic aspects of a product.

circulation
The number of copies of a published material that are sold to readers in a given period.

comic book artist
An individual who draws or illustrates characters and scenes in a comic book.

comic strip
An illustrated story in panels that is in newspapers or magazines.

consumer
A person who buys goods or services.

contract
An agreement written and signed by two or more people or businesses for the purpose of completing a specified task.

editor
A person in charge of a written material's publication.

editor-in-chief
The top editor in a publishing company.

freelance
The ability of a person to sell one's work while not being under contract by any employer.

Great Depression
The period in the 1930s of severe economic hardship in the United States.

invest
To put money into a business enterprise with the expectation of making a profit.

manufacturer
A person or group that produces goods from basic materials.

Marvel Method
The method of a comic book writer giving a basic story line to an artist and having the artist draw the comic book art before the writer puts in the text.

Norse
Relating to ancient Scandinavia.

psychiatrist
A doctor who treats patients who have psychiatric disorders.

publisher
The individual or group that prepares a written material for sale.

radiation
Energy emitted in rays or waves.

series
A story featuring particular characters that is told in installments over a long period of time.

speculator
A person who collects things to sell them for profit later.

superhero
A person or creature who fights evil and has abilities with extraordinary powers.

Viking
One member in a group of ancient Scandinavians who raided and invaded areas in northwestern Europe by ship.

villain
The evil character in any story that is motivated toward causing harm to others.

Source Notes

Chapter 1. The Turning Point
1. Jordan Raphael and Tom Spurgeon. *Stan Lee and the Rise and Fall of the American Comic Book*. Chicago: Chicago Review Press, 2003. 77.
2. Stan Lee and George Mair. *Excelsior! The Amazing Life of Stan Lee*. New York: Simon and Schuster, 2002. 113.

Chapter 2. Stanley and His Spaceship Bike
1. Stan Lee and George Mair. *Excelsior! The Amazing Life of Stan Lee*. New York: Simon and Schuster, 2002. 12–13.
2. Ibid. 10.
3. Jordan Raphael and Tom Spurgeon. *Stan Lee and the Rise and Fall of the American Comic Book*. Chicago: Chicago Review Press, 2003. 8.
4. Ibid.

Chapter 3. Planting the Seeds
1. Stan Lee and George Mair. *Excelsior! The Amazing Life of Stan Lee*. New York: Simon and Schuster, 2002. 30.

Chapter 4. Writer in War, Editor in Peace
1. Stan Lee and George Mair. *Excelsior! The Amazing Life of Stan Lee*. New York: Simon and Schuster, 2002. 32.
2. Jordan Raphael and Tom Spurgeon. *Stan Lee and the Rise and Fall of the American Comic Book*. Chicago: Chicago Review Press, 2003. 34.

Chapter 5. Trouble in Paradise
1. Stan Lee and George Mair. *Excelsior! The Amazing Life of Stan Lee*. New York: Simon and Schuster, 2002. 91.

Chapter 6. Soaring to Great Heights
1. Stan Lee and George Mair. *Excelsior! The Amazing Life of Stan Lee*. New York: Simon and Schuster, 2002. 121.
2. "Creating Spider-Man," *Stan Lee's Mutants, Monsters and Marvels*, Dir. Scott Zakarin. DVD. Sony Pictures/Creative Light, 2002.
3. Jordan Raphael and Tom Spurgeon. *Stan Lee and the Rise and Fall of the American Comic Book*. Chicago: Chicago Review Press, 2003. 71.
4. Mike DeLisa. "Some Thoughts on Some Thoughts on Blake Bell's Book, or Did Steve Ditko Once Play Baseball?" *20th Century Danny Boy*. 3 Aug. 2008. 9 Sept. 2008 <http://ohdannyboy. blogspot.com/2008/08/somethoughts-on-some-thoughts-on-blake.html>.
5. Stan Lee and George Mair. *Excelsior! The Amazing Life of Stan Lee*. New York: Simon and Schuster, 2002. 169.

Source Notes Continued

Chapter 7. The Marvel Age

1. Stan Lee and George Mair. *Excelsior! The Amazing Life of Stan Lee*. New York: Simon and Schuster, 2002. 172.

Chapter 8. Unhappy Promotion

1. Jordan Raphael and Tom Spurgeon. *Stan Lee and the Rise and Fall of the American Comic Book*. Chicago: Chicago Review Press, 2003. 125.
2. Stan Lee and George Mair. *Excelsior! The Amazing Life of Stan Lee*. New York: Simon and Schuster, 2002. 186.

Chapter 9. Branching Out

1. Stan Lee and George Mair. *Excelsior! The Amazing Life of Stan Lee*. New York: Simon and Schuster, 2002. 202–203.

Chapter 10. Takeover and a Smash Hit

1. Stan Lee and George Mair. *Excelsior! The Amazing Life of Stan Lee*. New York: Simon and Schuster, 2002. 215–216.
2. Jordan Raphael and Tom Spurgeon *Stan Lee and the Rise and Fall of the American Comic Book*. Chicago: Chicago Review Press, 2003. 197.

INDEX

INDEX CONTINUED

About the Author

Martin Gitlin is a freelance writer based in Cleveland, Ohio.
He has written more than a dozen educational books, including
biographies about NASCAR drivers Jimmie Johnson and Jeff
Gordon and historical books about the Battle of the Little Bighorn,
the stock market crash, and the landmark Brown v. Board of
Education Supreme Court decision. Gitlin has won more than
45 awards during his 25 years as a writer, including first place for
general excellence from the Associated Press. He lives with his wife
and three children in Ohio.

Photo Credits